PRONGHORNS

Tom Jackson

Grolier
an imprint of

www.scholastic.com/librarypublishing

Published 2008 by Grolier
An imprint of Scholastic Library Publishing
Old Sherman Turnpike, Danbury,
Connecticut 06816

For The Brown Reference Group plc
Project Editor: Jolyon Goddard
Copy-editors: Ann Baggaley, Lisa Hughes
Picture Researcher: Clare Newman
Designers: Jeni Child, Lynne Ross,
     Sarah Williams
Managing Editor: Bridget Giles

Volume ISBN-13: 978-0-7172-6279-3
Volume ISBN-10: 0-7172-6279-0

**Library of Congress
Cataloging-in-Publication Data**

Nature's children. Set 3.
    p. cm.
    Includes bibliographical references and
    index.
    ISBN 13: 978-0-7172-8082-7
    ISBN 10: 0-7172-8082-9
    1. Animals--Encyclopedias, Juvenile. 1.
    Grolier Educational (Firm)
    QL49.N384 2008
    590.3--dc22
                2007031568

Printed and bound in China

PICTURE CREDITS

Front Cover: **Nature PL**: Shattil and
Rozinski.

Back Cover: **Alamy**: Robert M. Vera;
Photolibrary.com: Erwin and Peggy Bauer,
Richard Kettlewell.

Corbis: W. Perry Conway 13, Darrell Gulin
21, 34 Charles Krebs 2–3, 30, D. Robert and
Lorri Franz 41; **FLPA**: David Hosking 37;
Nature PL: Niall Benvie 10, Thomas
Lazar 22, Shattill and Rozinski 18, 26–27,
38, 46; **NHPA**: Daniel Heuclin 6;
Photolibrary.com: Richard Kettlewell 9,
17, 42, 45, Barbara Von Hoffmann 14;
Shutterstock: Michael J. Thompson 4, 5, 29,
33.

Contents

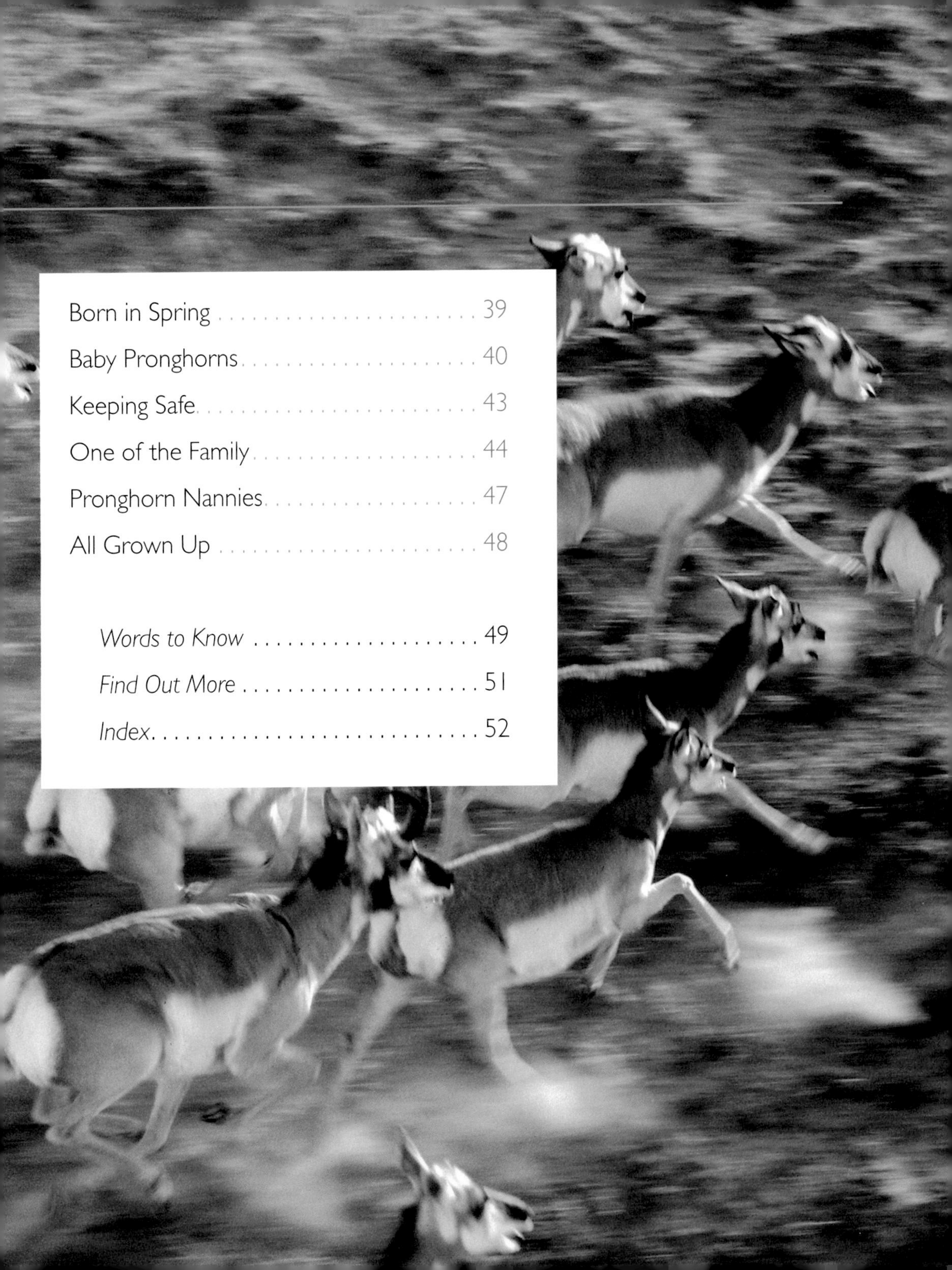

FACT FILE: Pronghorns

Class	Mammals (Mammalia)
Order	Even-toed hoofed mammals (Artiodactyla)
Family	Antilocapridae
Genus	*Antilocapra*
Species	Pronghorn (*Antilocapra americana*)
World distribution	North America
Habitat	Plains, deserts, and grassy foothills
Distinctive physical characteristics	Black branched horns with curved tips; short black mane and tan-colored coat with white at the throat and backside
Habits	Live in large herds; feed during the day
Diet	Grass, herbs, and leaves of shrubs

Introduction

Though it looks like it could be either, a pronghorn is neither a deer nor an antelope. In fact, the pronghorn is the only animal of its kind in the world. It is named for the branching horns that it carries on its head. Pronghorns live in the prairies of western North America and Mexico—and are perfectly adapted to life in open spaces. They are the fastest running mammals in North America, and can race for hours without getting tired. They also have extremely sharp eyesight, and can easily spot enemies in the far distance.

Pronghorns have curving, branched horns.

A young pronghorn gallops across an open prairie.

Born Free

The Blackfoot Native Americans have a story about the pronghorn. Legend has it that the Great Spirit, creator of the world, was looking for a place for pronghorns to live. He first put the animals on the mountains, but the land was too steep and rocky. He then let the pronghorns loose on the prairie. When he saw how they loved to run free, the Great Spirit realized that the open plain was the right home for them.

It is true that pronghorns really do like a lot of space to run. Soon after they are born, baby pronghorns can run faster than most dogs, even most horses! The young animals play running games. They race one another and trot around in circles. Even adult pronghorns often run just for the joy of it.

One of a Kind

There is nothing quite like a pronghorn. Pronghorns look similar to deer and antelope, and they live in much the same way as goats and cattle. But they are only distant relatives of these other animals.

Pronghorns belong to a group of **mammals** called the artiodactyls (AR-TEE-OH-DAK-TULS). These are animals with **hooves** that are split into an even number of toes. Like many other artiodactyls, the pronghorn has cloven hooves— that is, they are split into two toes. Artiodactyls include cattle, deer, pigs, camels, and antelope. Most of those animals belong to one of several large families. The pronghorn has a family, too, but it is the only member of its family. All its close relatives died out about five million years ago. The pronghorn is the only one of its kind.

The pronghorn family has a long history. Pronghorns are known to have been in existence at least 20 million years ago.

Standing in knee-high grasses, a pronghorn looks out over its prairie homeland.

Pronghorn Country

The pronghorn lives in North America. The animal is sometimes called the American antelope, even though it is not closely related to true antelope, which come from Africa and Asia. Most pronghorns are found in the western United States. They live on the Great Plains and in the Great Basin—a huge area of grasslands and shrubs that runs from southern Canada to northern Mexico.

At one time, tens of millions of pronghorns lived on the plains in enormous herds. From the 1800s onward, so many were shot by hunters that by the 1920s only a few thousand pronghorns remained. Since that time, control over hunting has become much stricter. And efforts to protect the pronghorn have helped its numbers to grow. About half a million of these animals now live in the wild. They stay far away from people and prefer the most remote places. Today, the most likely places to see a pronghorn are Montana or Wyoming.

Hoofed Cheetahs?

Pronghorns are built for speed. There is no other animal in North America that can run as fast as a pronghorn. Pronghorns can reach a top speed of about 60 miles (95 km) per hour. And they can jump nearly 20 feet (6 m) in a single bound! These animals can easily outrun wolves, deer, and even cougars. Many scientists think that there is only one land animal in the whole world that can travel faster. That is the cheetah, Africa's super-fast hunting cat.

People driving through the prairies sometimes get the chance to see just how fast a pronghorn can run. Sometimes pronghorns will race along the edge of the road, by the side of the car. After getting a good look at the car, they usually head back into the wilderness.

Pronghorns developed their speed millions of years ago as a way of escaping danger.

A pronghorn's slim legs don't look very powerful but the bones are extremely strong.

Speed Demons

Most hoofed animals, especially those with long, strong legs, can move very quickly. The pronghorn is no exception. In fact, it can easily outrun all other hoofed animals because its body is made in a very special way.

A pronghorn's hooves are extra wide to give it good grip as it pushes itself forward across the ground. The underside of the foot is covered in a thick bouncy pad. Those pads protect the pronghorn from jarring its legs as its feet pound the ground over and over again.

The pronghorn has a surprisingly sturdy body for such a fast animal. Adults grow to about 3 feet (1 m) at the shoulder. They weigh about 100 pounds (45 kg). The pronghorn's broad chest holds the animal's huge lungs and strong heart. A pronghorn is about the size of a sheep. But its heart can beat twice as fast as a sheep's to power the animal along at full speed.

Deep Breathing

A pronghorn is not just a very fast sprinter. It can keep up its speed for long distances without tiring. Running is hard work for any animal. A body needs a lot of oxygen to keep going. That is why people breathe quickly when they are running in a race. The oxygen helps the muscles work.

A pronghorn does not get tired easily, because its big lungs and wide windpipe allow it to take in very large breaths. That helps its muscles to work very quickly.

The pronghorn's stamina enables it to run a long way over even the most rugged ground.

Pronghorns' coat colors vary from light to dark tan. The buck, seen here, has black patches on his nose and below his jaw.

Hiding in the Grass

On the prairie, in every direction, there is nothing but grass and perhaps a tree or two. When a dangerous hunter, such as a cougar, comes looking for prey there are few places to hide. Small animals can dive into burrows under the ground. But if a large animal is under attack it can only run away, and that is what a pronghorn usually does.

Of course, pronghorns cannot spend all their time running. Luckily, they have another way of protecting themselves. Their gray and tan coat matches the colors of the grass around them. So when a pronghorn stands still, it almost disappears against the prairie background. This **camouflage** makes the animal more difficult for a hungry **predator** to see.

Comfortable Coat

A pronghorn's coat is not just good camouflage —it keeps the animal comfortable in all kinds of weather. The coat is made up of two layers of hairs. The hairs on the outside are long and thick. They are called **guard hairs**. As the name suggests, they protect the inner layer of hair, which is called the **underfur**. The underfur is made of much shorter hairs that are packed closely together. In winter, when cold winds blow across the plains, the pronghorn can flatten its guard hairs. The overlapping layers form a blanket that prevents the animal's body heat from escaping. In summer, when the prairie is hot, the pronghorn raises its guard hairs to let air flow around its body.

The underfur is thickest in winter. In spring, these hairs are shed and replaced by a thinner layer of hair. The shedding process takes a few weeks, and the pronghorn's coat looks untidy as the hairs fall away. In fall, a thicker coat grows back in preparation for the cold winter.

The hairs of a pronghorn's coat are hollow and filled with air. That helps keep the animal warm in winter.

Unlike antlers, horns do not usually branch. The pronghorn is the only animal to have branched horns.

Prongs and Spikes

It is easy to see how the pronghorn got its name. Its black **horns** branch to form two spikes, almost like the prongs of a pitchfork. One branch of the horn juts forward to a point. The other branch curves backward.

Male pronghorns, or **bucks**, have the largest horns. On some animals the horns grow to about 10 inches (25 cm) in length. During the mating season, bucks protecting their territory sometimes use their horns as weapons to drive away rivals. Female pronghorns, or **does**, have only small horns, or no horns at all.

Antlers or Horns?

A pronghorn's headgear is like that of no other animal. Deer, such as elk, caribou, and moose, grow antlers. Antlers are branches of hard bone that are shed each year and then grow back again. Animals like cattle, antelopes, and goats grow horns. Horns are also made from bone, but have a hard outer covering made of a substance called keratin. Hair, hooves, and fingernails are also made of keratin. True horns continue to grow from year to year and are never shed.

The pronghorn has bony horns covered with keratin, too. But unlike any other animal, it sheds the keratin covering every year so that it can be replaced with a new covering. The bone remains. The keratin takes about eight months to regrow and cover the bone again.

Black Eyes

The pronghorn's large black eyes can see a long way—as much as eight times as far as human eyes. When people want to look at distant objects, they use a pair of binoculars. The large lenses of binoculars collect a lot of light from the surroundings—more than human eyes can. The extra light helps people to see farther.

Pronghorns can see so far because their eyes work in the same way as the binoculars. The animals' eyes are huge. They are even bigger than those of a horse, which is a much larger animal than a pronghorn. Their big eyes collect enough light to see things more than a mile (1.6 km) away!

In winter pronghorns have
to travel long distances to
look for food.

Keeping Watch

Pronghorns live in the wide open prairie. They must always be on the lookout for approaching predators. If a pronghorn spots an enemy that is still a long way off, it will be able to get away with plenty of time to spare.

Once pronghorns have seen a predator they like to keep an eye on it. That way they know where it is all the time and the predator will not have a chance to sneak up behind the herd. Pronghorns sometimes follow a coyote as it hunts for prairie dogs or gophers. Most of the time, the pronghorns end up chasing the coyote away. However, they might also wait and watch to see if there are any more coyotes around. If several coyotes appear to be ganging up to make an attack, the pronghorns will probably run off.

Pronghorns like to know what is going on. They will approach a predator just to get a closer look.

The pronghorn
releases a special
warning smell from
its scent glands to tell
the herd to run away.

Time to Run

If a pronghorn senses danger it immediately tells the rest of the herd. It gives a snort that warns any pronghorns nearby. But it also needs to give a signal to other members of the herd that are farther away. The pronghorn sends out a message by raising the long white hairs on its rear end. The flash of white is easy to see in the sunshine—it is often called a "sun signal." Even animals a long distance away can spot the signal with their sharp eyes. Soon the whole herd is on the run.

Pronghorns make their escape together, running as a unified group. The group is led by a doe, while a large buck brings up the rear. He stays at the back to fight off a predator if it catches up.

Tasty Treats

Pronghorns are picky eaters. They tread carefully through the long grass looking for young shoots, tasty leaves, and sweet flowers to eat. In spring, they like to eat the new shoots of fresh grass. Their favorite summer foods are small herbs, such as clover, buttercups, and alfalfa. They are also fond of wild onions. In winter there are fewer choices. The pronghorns tend to eat the leaves of bushes, such as sagebrush.

Like deer and antelope, pronghorns chew the **cud**. Plant food is very tough to digest, so the pronghorns chew everything twice. The fresh food they swallow goes into the first part of their stomach. Here it is turned into a soft mass, or cud. The cud comes back up the throat into the pronghorn's mouth. The pronghorn chews the cud and its wide back teeth grind up the food even more. The pronghorn then swallows the cud again. This time, the cud goes farther down into the stomach and passes through the digestive system in the normal way.

It is common for a
pronghorn to lie
down while it
chews the cud.

A pronghorn searches among the snow for food.

Moving Around

Pronghorns could easily—and quickly—travel long distances if they wanted to, but they prefer to stay in one place. As long as there is enough food, the animals spend most of the year in an area about 16 square miles (40 sq km). However, in the last 100 or so years, the construction of fences, railroads, and roads that crisscross the prairie has made it difficult for the animals to go where they want. Pronghorns will not jump over even low fences, so they often find themselves trapped in one area.

In winter, pronghorns are forced to move greater distances. They head for the bottom of valleys, seeking shelter from bad weather. Eventually, even these areas are covered in snow and the pronghorns cannot find food. They then move again, heading for high ground. At higher altitudes, the strong winds blow away the snow, so the pronghorns can reach the grasses underneath.

Mating Dance

Pronghorns **mate** in late summer. At the start of the mating season, the bucks gather groups of does. Each group, or harem, contains about five or six does. Bucks attract the does' attention by performing a dance.

The dance starts with the buck opening his eyes so wide that they look like they are bulging out of his head. The buck then lowers his head and sways it from side to side. Next, he jumps to the left and then to the right. As he leaps, the buck ruffles his fur in waves down his back. If the does accept the buck's courtship they will stay with him to mate. Once the buck has collected his harem, he chases away any other bucks that come near.

This pronghorn buck has won his harem. If necessary, he will fight other bucks to protect it.

A baby pronghorn lies almost motionless until its mother returns.

Born in Spring

By early spring, pronghorn does are ready to give birth to their young. A doe does not build a nest or den. She finds a quiet spot away from the rest of the herd and gives birth out in the open. The best birthing places are among tall grasses and other plants. There the mother and her young can stay out of the sight of predators. Does most often give birth at night.

Most pronghorn does have twins. However, it is not unusual for a doe to give birth to just one or even three young pronghorns.

Baby Pronghorns

Baby pronghorns are called **kids**. Surprisingly, newborn kids weigh less than most newborn human babies. They are usually about 4½ pounds (2 kg). Some kids are half this weight. At birth, the kid appears to be all eyes and ears. Its spindly legs seem to be too long for its body.

As soon as the kid is born, its mother begins to lick it dry. The licking also wipes away much of the mother's smell. This stops predators, such as cougars and coyotes, from finding the baby by picking up its scent. Newborn pronghorn kids have very little smell of their own.

Only a few days old, and already on its feet, a young kid explores the prairie.

Male pronghorns play no part in caring for the young kids.

Keeping Safe

By the time a pronghorn kid is four days old it can already run faster than a horse. But it will be a few more weeks until the kid is strong enough to keep up with the adult pronghorns. Therefore, for the first week or two of its life, the kid stays in a special hiding place, or **cache**. Its mother chooses a cache in tall grasses or next to some rocks or a bush.

The mother does not stay in the cache with her young. A predator might follow her scent and find the hidden kid. Instead the mother keeps watch from a short distance away. She visits the kid several times a day to let it drink her milk. The kid does not eat anything else at this age. If a predator, such as a coyote, comes near the mother pronghorn tries to make it follow her away from the cache. If she is unsuccessful in drawing the predator's attention away from **her kid,** she will kick out at the enemy with her sharp hooves. That is usually enough to drive off the **hungry** predator.

43

One of the Family

After a week or two of hiding out in the cache, the pronghorn kid begins to make short trips away from its hiding spot. At three weeks old, the kid is strong enough to join the rest of the herd. The herd usually contains several does. All of them will have given birth to kids at about the same time. So many new kids join the herd.

The kids play together, running, prancing, and butting heads. These games are good exercise and help the kids grow stronger. The young pronghorns need to build up stamina for their life on the prairie.

Young pronghorns spend most of their time playing with other kids.

A "babysitter" takes charge of some youngsters and gives their mothers a break.

Pronghorn Nannies

When pronghorn kids are young, their mothers often share childcare with other does in the herd. One doe cares for all the youngsters, while the other mothers go off to rest and eat. A "nanny" can have as many as 12 kids to look after on her own. When the mothers return to the herd, their kids run to them. The young kids are hungry, too, and immediately begin drinking their mothers' milk.

By the time the young kids are a few weeks old they start eating grasses and shoots. But the kids continue to **nurse** until they are about five months old.

All Grown Up

Once the young kids stop drinking their mothers' milk, they begin to play less. They now behave more like the adult members of the herd. The youngsters stay with their mothers through the first winter. That is when they learn where to shelter from storms and where to find food in the snow.

In spring, their mothers give birth to more kids. The older offspring are left to look after themselves. By fall the kids are fully grown. They can mate and raise families of their own.

Life can be short for pronghorns. Some might not live more than one year. But others, if they are lucky, might run on the prairie until they are about ten years old.

Words to Know

Bucks   Male pronghorns.

Cache   Hiding place for a newborn
                   pronghorn.

Camouflage   Coloring that makes an animal hard
                   to see against its background. It
                   helps to protect the animal from
                   predators.

Cud   Swallowed food that is brought back
                   up into the mouth for chewing a
                   second time.

Does   Female pronghorns.

Guard hairs   Long hairs that make up the outer
                   layer of a pronghorn's coat.

Hooves   Feet of pronghorns, deer, and many
                   other animals. The hoof is really a
                   giant fingernail or claw.

49

Horns	A growth on a pronghorn's head made of bone with a hard, hollow cover over the top.
Kids	Young pronghorns.
Mammals	Animals that have hair and feed their young on milk.
Mate	To come together to produce young.
Nurse	To drink milk from a mother's body.
Predator	A hunting animal that kills other animals for food.
Underfur	A layer of short hairs next to the skin and underneath an outer coat of guard hairs.

Find Out More

Books

Frisch, A. *Pronghorns*. Kings of the Mountain. North Mankato, Minnesota: Smart Apple Media, 2002.

Medley, S. P. *Antelope, Bison, Cougar: A National Park Wildlife Alphabet Book*. El Portal, California: Yosemite Association, 2001.

Web sites

Pronghorn
www.enchantedlearning.com/subjects/mammals/pronghorn/Pronghorn.shtml
Information about pronghorns and a printout to color in.

Pronghorn Antelope
animals.nationalgeographic.com/animals/mammals/antelope.html
Key facts about pronghorns.

Index